International Trade

International Trade

Kenneth H. Smith

Associate Professor of Economics
Hunter College, City University of New York

Editorial Consultant: Marc Rosenblum

Lerner Publications Company—Minneapolis, Minnesota

j382   S65i

c.1

ACKNOWLEDGMENTS

The illustrations are reproduced through the courtesy of: pp. 8, 57, 76, Independent Picture Service; p. 10, Central Office of Information, London; pp. 11 (top), 12, 23, 28-29, 68-69, 71, 73, United Nations; p. 11 (bottom), Control Data Corporation; p. 17, Chase Manhattan Bank Money Museum; pp. 20, 30, Library of Congress; pp. 36-37, United States Bureau of the Mint; p. 39, Federal Reserve Bank of New York; p. 41, United States Department of Agriculture; p. 44, Bureau of Customs; p. 46, German Information Center; p. 47, Consulate General of Japan; p. 49, Eastman Kodak Company; p. 51, United States Navy; p. 63, Northwestern National Bank of Minneapolis; p. 64, Ramsey and Muspratt Ltd.

MAR 3 1 '71
CL

Contents

We must recognize that imports do not hurt us, but enrich us, both as individuals and as a nation. They bring us goods that we could not otherwise afford. They enable us to export an equal value of things we produce at a lower cost.

PAUL G. HOFFMAN

1

The Importance of
International Trade

Many Americans do not appreciate the importance
of international trade. The complex business of exports and imports, the balance of payments, and currency exchange may seem quite remote from daily
life. Actually, they are closely connected to many fa-
miliar aspects of life, such as the telephone, television,
chewing gum, and the coffee break. Foreign trade has
been an important economic activity in this country
since colonial times. American consumers have learned
to expect and appreciate imported goods, and the
United States has always earned some of its income
from selling goods abroad. Early exports were agricultural products, primarily tobacco, rice, and indigo. But

EXPORTS		IMPORTS	
COTTON	TRACTORS	BANANAS	WOOL
CARS	TOBACCO	TEA	CRUDE PETROLEUM

Some of the major United States exports and imports. Every country depends upon other countries for the goods it cannot grow or make. Also, countries depend upon the income they get from selling their own products overseas.

today the United States sells manufactured products as well, including plastics, jet aircraft, computers, and thousands of other products. Approximately six million persons are employed in industries which earn 10 percent or more of their profits from sales overseas.

Foreign trade is important to this country, but United States foreign trade is perhaps more important to the rest of the world. It accounts for some 20 percent of all international trade — more than any other single country. An increase or decrease in American foreign trade could have a serious impact on our trading partners. Many countries rely on foreign trade to supply 15 to 30 percent of their national income. However, the flow of international goods and services averages only 6 to 8 percent of the United States Gross National Product (GNP). Although the amount of American foreign trade is small when compared to the amount of domestic transactions, the items for which we trade are essential to our basic civilian and defense needs.

Interdependency

What becomes immediately apparent in looking at trade among nations is the fact of *interdependency*. No country can produce everything it needs; all countries must import goods. Imports help to maintain a nation's standard of living and promote its economic growth. Conversely, some percentage of the jobs and income within every country comes from export sales. These economic ties to the rest of the world cause individual nations to be concerned about the volume, composition, and patterns of international trade. Every nation wants to have a foreign economic policy which will enable it to benefit as much as possible from foreign trade.

One of the earliest concerns of economists was to explain how foreign trade could be used to the advantage of a particular political unit. The power of such ancient city-states as Athens and Carthage was in large part due to a successful trade policy. Trade ties were among the strongest links that held the empires of Rome and Charlemagne together. The desire for foreign products led Spain and England to the discovery and settlement of the American continents in

Beef from Argentina is loaded for shipment to Europe.

the fifteenth and sixteenth centuries. The need for
new raw materials and markets abroad brought about
the colonization of East Asia and Africa in the nineteenth century. Contact with the industrialized part
of the world and its modern production methods began the economic development of the new Asian and
African nations, which has been a major concern of
the 1960s.

Above: A car is sent from Great Britain to Australia.

Below: A computer is shipped from the United States to France.

International trade unites people from all over the world.

International trade has proved to be not only a source of goods and services, but also a channel for the exchange of ideas — and even people. Foreign commerce has hastened the spread of civilization and done much to bring together the different cultures of the globe. No better example of this is needed than the menu of a typical urban citizen who may within a week breakfast on bagels and coffee, snack on pizza and German beer, and dine on egg rolls and chop suey or tamales and enchiladas. The acceptance of foreign goods extends to almost every part of daily life. Clothing, furniture, toys, household goods, transistor radios, and automobiles often bear a label stating that they have been imported—made outside the United States.

Listed below are four concepts basic to an understanding of international trade. The following chapters discuss the economic principles from which these concepts are derived.

1. Nations trade to get the goods and services that they need and cannot produce at all, or only at great cost.

2. Goods will be traded that are in scarce supply or higher priced at home. They will be imported in quantities that are demanded and that can be paid for with the available supply of foreign money.

3. Goods will be imported if their price is equal to

or less than similar goods produced within the country. Often the selling price of the imported item will include an import tax as well as usual markups for profit and handling. Goods will be exported if their price is equal to or less than similar goods produced abroad.

4. Trade affects a country in two ways: Export sales, as well as money spent within the country by foreigners, create jobs and income at home. How much this affects the economy depends upon what percent of GNP is earned in international commerce. Secondly, imported goods contribute to a nation's economic well-being. If imports are of essential food products and materials necessary for industry, trade is very important; if imports are luxuries, a nation is less dependent on foreign trade.

2

Principles of Foreign Trade

Foreign transactions differ in many ways from domestic transactions — those carried out within a country's own borders. When nations are considering their foreign economic policy, and when they make international agreements to improve world trade, they are usually concerned with these differences.

The fact that exchange takes place across political boundaries is the first of these differences. There may be a tax collected at the boundary — a *tariff;* there may be a limit to the quantity of goods which can be imported or exported — a *quota;* there may be regulations known as "the invisible tariff" — red tape, long forms, inspections, or other complicated procedures that may make a transaction troublesome. These are basically *artificial barriers* set up at the national border by either one or both countries. Such barriers do not exist in domestic trade.

A second difference between foreign and domestic trade is monetary. Each nation has its own money, or *currency*, with its own denominations — dollars, pounds, marks, francs, pesos, lire, and a hundred or so others. An English merchant is not able to spend the dollars he earns from selling wool in this country to pay his bills in England; an American farmer cannot spend in this country the British pounds he earns from exporting wheat. In international trade each transaction really has two parts: the actual purchase of the item, and the purchase of foreign money *(foreign exchange)* to pay for it. For example, if you order an item selling for £1 (one pound) from London, you must first purchase an international money order for that amount. This costs approximately $2.40 plus a small charge. The price of English pounds, $2.40=£1, is known as the *exchange rate*, how much one country's currency is worth in terms of another.

Foreign commerce differs from domestic in a third way as well, known as *factoral immobility*. Within a country's borders the factors of production — labor, capital, technology, entrepreneurship, and title to land — can shift from one area to another without too much difficulty. Workers tend to move to those areas where wages are higher and labor is in short supply.

The British pound note, an East German deutschmark, a French five-franc piece, and a Mexican peso. Differences in currency make international trade more complicated than domestic trade.

Capital (money for investment) flows to those areas where interest rates and profits are more attractive. Technology (production know-how) and managerial talent follow the call of the most attractive income. Entrepreneurs, developers, and would-be property owners seek the location which will provide the best return.

Internationally, the factors of production cannot move easily from one country to another. Tourists are generally welcome, but extra workers may not be. A foreigner is often required to have a special work permit before he can take a job. Capital investment is sought by many nations, but often these nations limit the kind and amount of investment they will allow. Also, many nations do not like foreign control of their own enterprises. This applies not only to capital investments, but also to ownership of land. Patents and licenses may protect an inventor within his own country, but they may not guarantee him protection outside. What factoral immobility means is that international boundaries represent an obstacle, or even a barrier, to the free flow of productive factors from areas of abundance to areas of shortage.

Finally, there are differences between domestic and foreign trade which economists label *socio-cultural* — differences in language, laws, and trading customs. These keep economic transactions from being as simple or uniform as they might be within a single country. The problem of communicating in different tongues often makes foreign trade difficult. Variations in laws and in business practices can also interfere with the easy exchange of goods and services.

Specialization and Free Trade

Economic theorists have focused on the first two of the differences between foreign and domestic trade, artificial barriers and money systems. There are few issues upon which there is such agreement among economists as this aspect of international trade theory. Economists are convinced that all artificial trade barriers should be removed, and that all monetary systems should be coordinated. They recommend that international transactions be as much like domestic ones as possible.

Economists make this unanimous recommendation because it is a way to solve one of mankind's persistent problems: how to produce enough goods to satisfy human needs from the relatively limited resources available. The purpose of international trade theory is to show how the world's resources can be used most effectively, to produce the greatest output of goods and services for all nations. This goal can be accomplished by extending to the international sphere some of the ideas which led to the development of the free enterprise system in Western countries. Like so many of the most durable economic laws, these ideas were first brought together in Adam Smith's book, *The Wealth of Nations* (1776).

Smith published this book in a time when the

Adam Smith. In The Wealth of Nations *Smith argued against tariffs and other restrictions on free trade.*

theory of *mercantilism* was popular. This theory was based on the idea that each country should collect as much gold, silver, precious gems, and furs as possible. This would be achieved, said the mercantilists, when a country always sold more abroad than it imported. This condition, having more exports than imports, was labeled a *favorable balance of trade.* When a country imported more than it exported, it was considered to have an *unfavorable balance of trade.* (Today, economists still use these phrases, but they no longer use them to indicate that such a balance is really "good" or "bad" for the country's economy.) The mercantilists also argued that government should control the economy and do everything in its power to promote export trade. They expected the government to establish protective tariffs, build port facilities, keep wages down so that prices would be low, help finance shipbuilding, and furnish naval protection for merchant ships.

Adam Smith, David Hume, and other classical economists disagreed with mercantilistic policies and supported a policy of free trade — trade without artificial barriers or governmental control. They argued that a treasury filled with money wasn't worth very much if there were no goods to spend it on. They also pointed out that it was not likely that every nation could maintain a "favorable balance of trade" at the same time. The object of foreign trade was not to collect wealth, but to get goods as cheaply as possible and in the quantities needed. The economists claimed that a favorable balance of trade actually may fail to benefit a country's economy. They based their arguments on these two ideas: First, the wealth of a nation is not in its money, but in its goods and its capacity to produce them; second, specialization and free trade lead to greater output and lower prices for all countries.

It is not difficult to understand the first idea. Money is valuable only because it can buy goods and services. One cannot eat or wear money. The second concept is somewhat less simple. The basic case for specialization in international trade is that each economy is well equipped to turn out some products more efficiently, and therefore more cheaply, than others. This is because each country is unique; it has a different combination of land, labor, capital, technology, and entrepreneurship, and it also has different climate and geographical conditions. In addition to these separate characteristics, each nation is different in its size, location, and national customs and traditions.

Specialization in its purest form is illustrated by the concept of *absolute advantage*. This means that one country can produce something, because of its combination of resources, that few other economies can produce at all, or that they can produce only at an extremely high cost. It can be said that the Union of South Africa, the Soviet Union, and the state of Arkansas share absolute advantage in the production of diamonds. Similarly, the United States enjoys an absolute advantage in the production of automobiles in relation to Costa Rica, but the latter country has an absolute advantage over the United States in coffee.

There seems to be little room for arguing against the free trade of goods which every nation cannot produce. When a country has absolute advantage in a product, other countries must import to obtain that product. By the same token, this country is not able to turn out every product it requires, and it too must import.

A worker picks coffee on a plantation in Costa Rica. Costa Rica and other Latin American countries have an absolute advantage over the United States in producing coffee.

23

A variation of absolute advantage and the basis of the argument for free trade is the concept of *comparative advantage*. When several countries can produce the same item, some can usually produce it at lower costs than others. The countries which produce the item at lowest cost of resources and manpower are said to have a comparative advantage. Economists recommend that each economy specialize in producing those items for which it has comparative advantage. It should then trade the surplus it produces for other items which can be produced elsewhere more cheaply.

To illustrate the advantages of specialization, let us assume that in the United States 100 units of land, labor, capital, technology, and entrepreneurship can be put together in such a way as to produce *either* 30 automobiles *or* 100 bicycles in a week's time. In the United Kingdom (Great Britain) 100 units of the same resources can produce 25 automobiles *or* 115 bicycles in a week. In this example the United States and the United Kingdom are both able to produce automobiles and bicycles, but each enjoys a different comparative advantage. The United States can produce automobiles more efficiently; Great Britain can produce bicycles more efficiently. If these two countries did not specialize, and they used 200 resource units for making bicycles *and* automobiles, their production would be as follows:

	Automobiles[1]	Bicycles[1]
U.S.	30	100
U.K.	25	115
Total	55	215

[1]Output per 100 resource inputs per week.

If, however, each of these economies used its 200 resource units for only that product it could turn out more efficiently, the total production for both items would be greater. This is the result of specialization.

	Automobiles[1]	Bicycles[1]
U.S.	60	0
U.K.	0	230
Total	60	230

[1]Output using 200 resource inputs per week.

Thus the greater the degree of specialization, the larger will be the total output of goods and services from the world's resources.

Since, in the example, the United States would have produced no bicycles, and the United Kingdom would have no automobiles, they would have to trade to get them. The United States will sell no more than 30 of its 60 automobile output, because 30 is the amount it would have produced without specialization and trade. Nor will the United Kingdom sell more than 115 of its 230 bicycles, for if it did, there would be no benefit. But notice the difference. Now it is possible for the United States to have 30 cars and *more than* 100 bicycles, just as it is now possible for the United Kingdom to have 115 bicycles and *more than* 25 automobiles. There are five additional automobiles and 15 extra bicycles to bargain for.

Exactly how many bicycles the United States will buy and how many automobiles the United Kingdom will buy depends on many factors, including the demand for automobiles and bicycles in the two countries, their ability to pay for the imports, and the prices of each. Trade may adjust, for example, so that the United States will keep 33 cars and buy 105 bicycles, and the United Kingdom will have 125 bicycles and buy 27 automobiles. Both economies have benefited. Just where the bargain will be struck is called the *terms of trade* — the amount of money one nation receives for its exports compared to the money it will spend for its imports. When the terms of trade are equal, a nation pays the same amount of money for the goods it imports as it pays to produce the goods it exports in exchange.

In the long run, as each nation specializes in producing items for which it has comparative advantage, and free trade becomes widespread, there is a tendency for the terms of trade to equalize. In the example above, in the long run, the terms of trade would tell us that the cost of producing 27 automobiles in the United States was roughly the same as the cost of producing 105 bicycles in the United Kingdom. Until artificial barriers to trade are removed, and specialization is complete, however, the terms of trade will not be of equal value.

Since there are more than two countries and two products in international trade, is the theory of comparative advantage invalid? Not at all. Even though a single economy may have a comparative advantage for a product, it will not be possible for it to supply that product to the entire world. A country may have limited resources available within its borders. This will tend to raise production costs, cut the advantage, and make it necessary for other nations to produce. Also, a comparative advantage may exist at the place of production, but the costs of packaging, freight, and handling may reduce the advantage over long distances. This may allow producers nearer to some markets to enjoy a comparative advantage over more distant, more efficient producers.

Even with perfect specialization, nations would still produce a variety of products. If there is free trade, there will be many commodities and many producers in international markets, and they will compete against each other. Each nation will try to offer buyers better and cheaper goods. This competition forces each country to use its resources even more efficiently. Artificial barriers and other obstacles to specialization and free trade tend to reduce the quantity and variety of goods available to mankind.

Sugar from Peru is unloaded from a ship on Lake Titicaca and placed on a train for cities in Bolivia. Because it can transport sugar so easily, Peru has a comparative advantage in sugar over countries in North America and Europe.

John Stuart Mill. He observed that under ideal conditions of specialization and free trade nations would be so dependent upon each other that they would not be able to wage war.

While no economist expects total specialization and completely free trade to appear in the foreseeable future, every step in that direction means more material goods for everyone. John Stuart Mill, an economist who lived in the middle of the nineteenth century, concluded that with specialization and free trade it would be almost impossible for nations to wage war. Every nation would be dependent upon imports; no nation would have enough resources for prolonged conflict.

3

The Balance of Payments

Economists have developed the balance of payments statement to keep track of transactions in international trade. This statement is a financial report, issued by each country, showing its exchanges with the rest of the world. It records the amount of money which is exchanged when the country buys or sells goods and services, and also the amount of money which is exchanged in purely financial transactions (such as loans or investments). When a country has taken in as much money as it has spent, it has an *equilibrium* in its balance of payments. If it takes in more than it spends, or spends more than it takes in, it has a disequilibrium in its balance of payments. To understand the nature of the payments system and the meaning of disequilibrium, it is necessary to examine the structure of the balance of payments statement.

Table One

United States Balance of Payments, 1967 and 1968

(amounts given in billions of dollars)

	1967	1968
Current Account		
Exports	+ $45.8	+ $50.6
Imports	− 41.0	− 48.1
Net Trade Balance	+ 4.8	+ 2.5
Capital Account		
Transfers		
government	− 2.2	− 2.1
private	− 0.8	− 0.8
Loans and Investments		
government	− 2.0	− 0.4
private	− 2.8	+ 1.6
Net Capital Balance	− 7.8	− 1.7
Preliminary Balance (Current Account minus Capital Account)	− 3.0	+ 0.8
Errors and Omissions	− 0.5	− 0.7
Final Net Balance of Payments	− $ 3.5	+ $ 0.1

Source: U.S. Department of Commerce

Table One shows the United States payments statements for 1967 and 1968.

The first part of the balance of payments statement is called the *current account*. It lists the flow of money resulting from sales to, or purchases from, foreign countries: exports and imports of merchandise, earnings and expenses on tourist travel, on transportation, and on similar services. Whenever an exchange brings money into the country (when another country buys an export product), it is entered in the current account as a credit (plus). When an exchange takes money out of the country (when a product is imported), it is entered as a debit (minus). This is true whether the money is paid by an individual, a business firm, or the government. If the total credits are greater than the total debits, there is a surplus in the current account. The country has done more exporting than importing. This is known as an export balance of trade. Table One shows that the United States had a net export surplus in 1967 and 1968. When a country has imported more than it has exported, the debits exceed the credits, and there is a deficit, or an import balance of trade.

The surplus or deficit in the current account is not the same as a surplus or deficit in a country's total balance of payments. A country may, for example, have a surplus in the current account and still have a deficit in its balance of payments, as the United States did in 1967. (See Table One.) This is possible because a country's balance of payments is determined not only by its exports and imports, but also by the amount of capital that comes in and goes out of the country.

There are many transactions among nations which involve only capital, in which there is no exchange of goods or services. These include private and government loans, grants, investments, the purchase and sale of bonds and stocks, as well as gifts and pensions. All of these transactions are entered in the *capital account* on the balance of payments statement.

When money is given to a foreign government or citizen as a gift, grant, donation, or pension, it is entered as a debit in the capital account. Direct gifts of money are called unilateral transfers. Unilateral transfers are "one-way" transfers; the money has not been loaned or invested, and it will not be paid back to the country.

When money is loaned, borrowed, or invested, it also is entered in the capital account. Money loaned to a foreign government or citizen is recorded as a debit, because purchasing power has left the economy. The money has literally been exported. But loans are not unilateral transfers of money; interest and principal (the amount loaned) will eventually be repaid. When repayment does occur, the inflow of capital and the interest it has earned is entered as a credit in the capital account. Similarly, when money is borrowed from a foreign country, it is entered as a credit in the capital account. When the money and its interest are paid back to the foreign country, they are entered as a debit.

This system accurately shows the movement of capital resources in and out of the country, but it does not indicate that money flowing abroad is usually paid out for an asset of equal value. The asset may be a bond, a promise to pay, securities, or ownership of some property. Thus the capital account may show an overall debit, or imbalance, but United States citizens have actually gained real assets. Another factor which makes the capital account somewhat inaccurate is that loans or purchases of stock are made in large lump sums, whereas repayments, with interest or dividends, return at a slower pace and in smaller amounts. The large sums show up immediately as debits; the repayments (the credits) appear gradually in later years.

In addition to accounting for goods and services (in the current account) and capital flow (in the capital account), the balance of payments statement attempts to allow for unrecorded transactions in the section labeled *errors and omissions*. The estimates of unreported exchanges in this section are based on the amount of foreign money held by American financial institutions. If banks and investment companies have less foreign money than the current and capital accounts indicate, for example, the errors and omissions section will indicate that a larger amount of United States money has actually been spent in foreign countries.

Totaling all three accounts gives a picture of a nation's economic position in relation to the rest of the world during a given time period. It shows how the nation is doing in its foreign trade. Data (information) on the balance of payments is collected and published each month and each quarter of the year. The most important set of figures, however, is the annual (yearly) balance of payments statement. It may show, for example, a surplus in the current account, which may be erased by a deficit in the capital account, as Table One indicates happened in the United States in 1967. Or, the statement may show a surplus or deficit in both accounts. It is the overall picture that is important for a nation. If a country takes in

The Fort Knox Depository, Kentucky. A large amount of the United States gold stock is stored here. The Federal Reserve Banks may remove gold from Fort Knox if it is needed to settle a deficit in the United States balance of payments.

from abroad more money than it spends, there is a surplus in the balance of payments and a surplus of foreign money in the country. If the statement shows that more money has been spent overseas than has been taken into the economy, there is a deficit in the balance of payments.

In official publications of the balance of international payments there is generally a settlement account, an added table of data showing how the nation has made up for its surplus. This entry indicates a transfer of funds from one country to another. If a country has an overall deficit, the settlement account shows that gold, securities, and bonds have left the country, and that foreign bank accounts within the country have increased. If a country has a surplus, this transfer account records an inflow of gold or other international reserves, increased holdings of foreign securities and bonds, and larger bank accounts held by the nation's citizens overseas.

The balance of payments situation between France and the United States serves as a good example of how payments deficits are settled. Throughout most of the 1960s the United States had large trade deficits with France. At the end of each year, primarily because of tourism and imports, French merchants had more dollars than they could use; there was an excess of dollars within France. The merchants traded their dollars at the French central bank, which gave them francs for their dollars according to the official exchange rate. The French central bank then asked the United States central bank (the Federal Reserve Bank) to exchange the dollars for gold. The official monetary price of gold is $35 per ounce; for each $35 held by the French central bank, the United States paid one ounce of gold. Until the late 1960s (when France began to have an increase in imports), the United States transferred millions of dollars' worth of gold to France each year.

Thus, the balance of payments statement always balances even if there is a surplus or deficit, because such a surplus or deficit is financed by an inflow or

outflow of an equal amount of *international liquidity*. International liquidity is money that is acceptable to all nations — gold, United States dollars, or British pounds sterling. Promises to pay from reliable credit sources, such as governments or international agencies, also serve as international liquidity.

In the long run, then, an economy must maintain an equilibrium in its international transactions with the rest of the world. Too many deficits over several years will completely use up a country's gold reserves and its credit. Too many years of surpluses will increase the amount of money and liquidity within the nation, and this may cause inflation at home. This is because, generally speaking, a large amount of money in circulation tends to increase economic activity and raise prices and wages.

Whenever there is disequilibrium in its balance of payments, either surplus or deficit, a nation immediately looks for the cause. Is it too few exports or too many imports? Have investment funds been placed overseas because they can make more money there than at home? What about government lending and spending overseas?

The source of disequilibrium might be *temporary*. A poor crop year may reduce a nation's agricultural exports and perhaps cause it to import more. An especially good crop year may have the opposite effect. A series of strikes during one year may reduce exports and increase imports. Temporary difficulties are often

Corn damaged by corn borers. Widespread crop damage in one year may reduce a nation's exports or cause it to import more during that year. The resulting deficit in the balance of payments is only temporary; next year's crop may be plentiful.

left to adjust themselves over a period of time.

Sometimes a nation imports more than is typical because of inflation of domestic prices (possibly because of payments surplus). High domestic prices also cause a decrease in exports; foreign nations buy fewer of the country's goods. Perhaps a nation sells less overseas because its trading partners themselves are undergoing an economic slowdown or are short of foreign exchange. Or it may sell more overseas because other countries are experiencing inflation. Sometimes a nation is able to export less because its production is inefficient, and its prices are therefore too high to compete in the world market. These kinds of disequilibrium are labeled *cyclical* and they are of internal origin. These conditions respond to monetary or fiscal policy adjustments in the countries in which they occur. Adjustments to curb inflation or increase efficiency are the responsibility of those countries.

Long run imbalances are more serious; they imply that something is fundamentally wrong with a nation's economic relations with the rest of the world. If the difficulty arises in the current account, it may indicate that the country is losing markets abroad because of technological backwardness (it lacks the production methods to use its resources correctly). A long run imbalance may show that a country's exports are no longer attractive in the world market, or that it is getting more competition from other nations. The problem may be in the capital account. It could be an outflow of capital because investors can make higher profits and interest rates in other countries. It may be large government expenditures overseas for military or political purposes. When there is such a *fundamental* disequilibrium, or as it is sometimes called, a *structural* disequilibrium, a basic change in economic policy is required.

United States Balance of Payments

A look at the balance of payments experience of the United States over the last several years offers a good example of the kind of changes that affect equilibrium. The United States had enjoyed export surpluses in the current account in every year since 1873.

Table Two

United States Balance of Payments, 1957-1968

(amounts given in billions of dollars)

Year	Amount of Deficit or Surplus
1957	$ + 0.6
1958	− 3.4
1959	− 3.9
1960	− 3.9
1961	− 2.4
1962	− 2.2
1963	− 2.7
1964	− 2.8
1965	− 1.3
1966	− 1.4
1967	− 3.5
1968	+ 0.1

Source: U.S. Department of Commerce

Thus there was surprise and concern when small deficits in the balance of payments in the early 1950s grew from 1958 to 1968 into annual deficits averaging about $3 billion. During this time the gold stock of $21 billion shrank to a little less than $11 billion; the United

United States citizens returning from overseas go through customs in San Francisco. American tourists go abroad in greater numbers than foreign citizens visit the United States.

States paid $10 billion to other countries to finance its deficits. The balance of payments statements point up three main causes of this dramatic shift:

1. The export surplus in the current account has narrowed from some $6 billion to a little over $1 billion. Imports have grown at faster rates than exports. The gap in tourism has widened; American tourists have gone overseas in greater numbers than tourists have come to the United States.

2. Private capital investments overseas have increased because of profitable markets and the advantages to be gained from branch operations.

3. The government has continued to spend large amounts of money for foreign aid and military and defense purposes.

Underlying these changes are a number of important developments at home and overseas. Inflation within the country has raised the price of American exports and therefore made them less competitive. (The price rise in the United States, however, has been less than in many other industrial nations.) Japan and Western Europe not only have fully recovered from the destruction of World War II, but they also have modernized and achieved productivity equal to and greater than the United States in many products. This has gained comparative advantage for them

A converter ring manufactured in West Germany. These rings are made to hold large cylinders containing molten iron.

and meant a loss of sales for the United States.

For many years the United States did have a large trade surplus in the current account. It was large enough to make up for the money spent on foreign aid and the capital invested abroad by private citizens. But in the 1950s the export surplus grew much smaller. At the same time, the United States had slightly higher capital outflows. These two factors resulted in a series of disequilibria on the deficit side.

This condition continued until 1968. In that year there was a small surplus in the United States balance of payments. This surplus was brought about by several measures: a drastic reduction of government loans and spending, strict guidelines limiting private lending and investing abroad, and requests that American corporate profits from overseas be returned to United States banks. These measures, added to an early repayment of loans by several foreign governments and an increase of investment by foreign citizens in United States securities, produced a small surplus — about $100,000,000. (See Table One.) The

A sewing machine assembly line in Japan. Both Japan and West Germany have become highly industrialized since World War II.

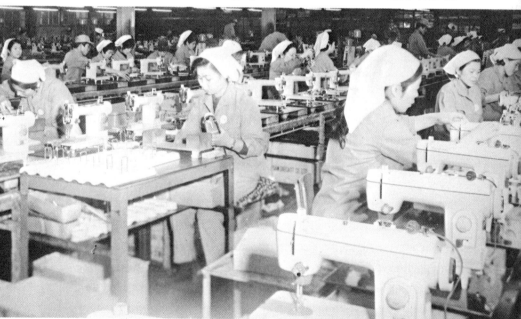

export balance of trade, however, continued to shrink. Because the events of 1968 were special conditions which are unlikely to be repeated, the basic causes of the United States balance of payments deficits still have not been removed.

What must be done to give the United States equilibrium in its balance of payments? Can corrections be made within the framework of specialization and free trade?

Clearly the United States needs to restore a comfortable surplus in the balance of trade; there must be enough surplus in the current account to make up for deficits in the capital account. To achieve this, the United States must regain comparative advantage and sell more abroad than it has in recent years. We must at least have an increase in exports equal to the increase in imports. International trade theory shows that the United States must have greater economic efficiency and lower prices in order to have comparative advantage. The real cures for the export problem are using modern production techniques, keeping wages and profits from increasing faster than productivity, and selling American products more forcefully. Protective devices (such as tariffs), and government subsidies (money given to industries) may give temporary relief to the balance of trade problem by reducing imports. But they hide the lack of efficiency and

Tourists in front of the Jefferson Memorial, Washington, D.C. An increase in the number of tourists to the United States would help lower the deficit in the United States balance of payments.

ultimately will not create a genuine trade advantage.

Boosting the balance of trade also requires a greater use of United States shipping, air freight, insurance, and other trade services, as well as an increase in the number of tourists to the United States. Avoiding inflation at home is also essential if our export prices are to be kept low and thus accurately reflect any new efficiencies achieved.

To reduce the deficit in the capital account, the United States must maintain a growth rate in its economy which will attract both domestic and foreign capital investment.

Several factors will, in the years ahead, give some relief to the United States payments problem in the capital account. One of these factors is the repayment of the private capital outflow of the last decade. United States dollars loaned and invested by private citizens are beginning to return with their dividends and interest. These repayments will be added to the credit column. Another factor is the gradual repayment of loans which were made by the government to other countries. Moreover, the outflow of new government lending is considerably smaller.

For the past few years, American economic aid to developing countries has become increasingly *tied*. That is, money loaned abroad can be spent only on United States goods and services. This makes up for the outflow of loaned funds with a balancing purchase of American exports. In addition, more and more nations are sharing with the United States the burden of providing capital to the less developed regions of the world.

Military and defense spending has been a consistent drain on the capital account in the United States balance of payments. Although this spending is a relatively small percentage of the total outlay, less than 10 percent over the last 10 years, the United States

Navy fighter planes. Military and defense spending overseas has contributed to the deficit in the United States balance of payments.

needs surpluses of $5 to $6 billion in the current account to make up for this outflow. Two prospects seem inevitable. Either the United States must reduce its commitments to protect the noncommunist world, or other free nations must assume a larger share of the costs. A third alternative is increasingly a possibility, but it depends on scientific and political breakthroughs. The world may achieve some degree of disarmament and the ability to maintain enough defense capabilities without overseas bases.

Further complicating the United States balance of payments problem is the continued existence of trade barriers, many of which discriminate against American goods. Many of these restrictions were set up in the worldwide depression of the 1930s and the immediate post-World War II years. During these difficult times, nations were trying to keep their gold reserves and to promote their domestic industries. Now, such barriers are no longer needed. The removal of these special taxes, currency controls, quotas, and invisible tariffs not only would aid the United States, but it would also benefit all trading nations. Each nation would be forced to develop those products in which it has a comparative advantage. Competition would increase, keeping prices low and causing nations to use their resources with greater efficiency. Removing the trade barriers would hurt the industries making the goods which are now protected, and it may be necessary to give them some aid so they can adjust, but the increased specialization and better resource use would provide important long run gains.

The benefits provided by free trade policy are not based on theory alone; they have been proven in actual experience in the United States, the European Common Market, and other regional trade associations — all of which will be discussed in the pages ahead.

In sum, economic theory does offer solutions to the problem of payment deficits. They may not be the easiest or most obvious policies, nor are they likely to please everyone in the economy. Their value is that they go to the causes of the problem; they do not attempt to do away with the symptoms, as restrictive trade practices do. They require a greater amount of international cooperation, and they emphasize the fact that to achieve maximum efficiency of resource use and greatest world output, there must be specialization and a recognition of economic interdependence among all nations.

4

The International
Monetary System

When the balance of payments records a nation's transactions with the rest of the world, it does so in money terms. As we have seen, when there is a deficit or a surplus, there must be a transfer of international liquidity — funds that are acceptable as payment among all nations. Also, when citizens or business firms sell abroad, they generally want payment in their own currency. Making international payments between nations or between persons requires a complicated system that will determine how much one currency is worth in terms of others. Over the past hundred years three major systems have been used to settle the problem of international exchange: the gold standard, fluctuating rates, and fixed or pegged par values.

Gold Standard

The gold standard was developed just before the turn of the century, and it lasted until the late 1920s. Nations using the gold standard would set the value of their own currencies in terms of how many grains of fine gold they were worth. The dollar, for example, was defined as 28 8/10 grains of gold. One country's currency could be exchanged for another on the basis of how much gold one contained in relation to the other; gold acted as the common denominator. Nations agreed to buy or sell gold at their central bank or treasury at its market price, and they allowed gold to be freely imported and exported. All these nations used either gold coins for currency, or gold as a backing for their paper currency, so that the quantity of gold reserves on hand affected the available supply of money and credit. When a nation's gold reserves increased or decreased, the amount of money it had in circulation changed accordingly.

Under the gold standard system a balance of payments disequilibrium was settled by a transfer of gold from one country to another. The advantage of the gold standard system was that it tended to force each nation to keep its trade in balance. Whenever a country had a trade deficit (its imports were greater than its exports), it would make up the deficit with gold, and the supply of gold within the country would decrease. The smaller gold reserves would make less money available within the country, and this would ultimately make prices lower. As soon as prices were lower, that country's products would sell better on the world market. This would automatically correct the trade deficit; other nations would import more products. They would then be forced to give up some of their gold reserves. Conversely, if a country exported more than it imported, gold would flow in, reserves would rise, and with them, money supply and prices. This would make the nation's products higher priced and therefore less attractive in world markets, and its exports would fall. This system was labeled the *price-specie-flow* mechanism. A change in price would cause a flow of specie (in this instance gold), which would tend to equalize prices and adjust the balance of trade.

The whole gold standard mechanism was very appealing because it supposedly operated without policy changes and in response to market forces. It did work successfully so long as there were only a few major trading nations whose gold reserves were roughly in proportion to the amount of trade, and each of the countries played by the rules of the system.

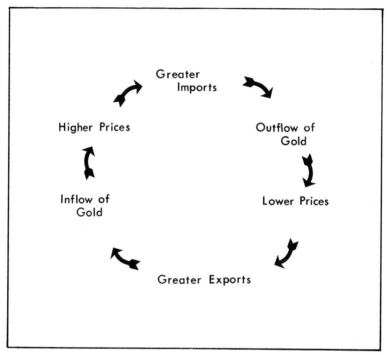

The price-specie-flow mechanism.

World War I redistributed gold reserves. More nations, many without any reserves to speak of, began to engage in international commerce. To protect their reserves, they broke the rules of the gold standard system. Furthermore, countries were no longer willing to undergo a price decline and recession, which caused unemployment and discontent, merely to bring trade into balance. As nations placed restrictions on gold purchases, and on gold export and import, and as they failed to keep their money supply in proportion to their gold reserves, the system broke down.

The gold bullion reserve standard took the place of the gold standard. Some countries, instead of having their own gold reserves, used strong currencies of other countries. The British pound sterling, the French franc, and the United States dollar, all of which could be converted into gold, were kept as reserves by many nations.

Fluctuating Rates

After the great stock market crash of 1929, which was followed by the worldwide depression, international trade almost collapsed under successive waves of tariffs, quotas, and exchange controls. These were enacted to protect domestic products from foreign competition so that each nation's economy could recover from depression. Until World War II broke out, exchange rates were, for the most part, allowed to fluctuate (change) freely in the international money markets of New York, London, Paris, and Shanghai. The exchange rate of one currency in terms of another was determined by the forces of supply and demand. Under the economic law of supply and demand, when an item is scarce, the demand is greater than the supply, and the price goes up. On the other hand, if the supply is greater than the demand, the price will fall.

When French francs were in short supply, in New York, let us say, their price in dollars would rise, and the purchaser would get fewer francs per dollar; if they were plentiful in Rome, it would be possible to exchange a dollar for more francs than in New York.

The principal trading powers kept their currencies near an official exchange rate, so that their trading partners could rely on the price of their currency. They controlled the price through exchange stabilization operations. Representatives of the country's central banks would watch the price of its currency in major money markets. If the exchange rate fell, and the money was getting too cheap (too far below the official rate), the exchange stabilization representative would go into the market and buy up the currency — with gold if necessary — until an artificial shortage was created. This brought the exchange rate back to the desired level. Should a currency in short supply become too expensive (exchanged at a rate above the official level), the exchange stabilization representative would sell his nation's currency at lower and lower rates until the supply was increased and an acceptable reduction in price had been made. These stabilization activities tended to keep key currencies at the same price. These activities also tended to stabilize the currencies of countries which used the key currencies as reserves.

International trade was disturbed in the late 1920s

and 1930s not only by the depression, but also by widespread use of "beggar-thy-neighbor" policies and competitive devaluation. Many countries attempted to solve their own internal economic difficulties at the expense of their trading partners. They enacted high tariffs on imports, gave subsidies to exporters, and began drives for national self-sufficiency. They also dumped surplus production in world markets at prices lower than at home, and drew up sets of multiple exchange rates to make their currency cheaper for some nations than for others.

In order to gain further advantage, or at least maintain a large share of existing export markets, nations engaged in competitive devaluation. One nation would devalue its currency, and other nations would in turn make equal or greater devaluations. Changing foreign exchange rates has long been a method of correcting or improving an economy's balance of payments.

Devaluation is making a country's currency cheaper in terms of other currencies. Given a period of time for other nations to adjust, and depending on the demand for a nation's exports, devaluation tends to increase sales abroad and cut back imports. For example, before the British devaluation of 1968, £1 was exchanged on the international money market for $2.80; after devaluation £1 was worth $2.40. Devaluation did not appreciably change prices of domestic products sold within the country, but it made British goods and services less expensive in the world market. It also made the goods of other nations more expensive for British citizens. If a Briton wanted to buy an American product priced at $2.80, it cost him £1 before devaluation; afterward the same product cost him one pound, 3 shillings, 4 pence. If an American wanted to buy a British product priced at £1, it cost him $2.80 before devaluation, but only $2.40 afterward.

Evaluation, making a country's currency more expensive in relation to others, has the opposite effect. Foreign monies, and consequently foreign goods, become less expensive to citizens of the evaluating country, thus increasing imports. The country's exports rise in price because the price of the nation's money is higher. For example, in 1959, $1.00 would buy 4 West German deutschmarks; earlier, in 1958, $1.00 could purchase 4 marks, 20 pfennigs. Evaluation in this instance meant that German goods which could have been bought for 25¢ now cost foreigners 30¢.

During the depression many countries tried to improve their trade by devaluating their currencies. But this reduction was matched by other nations, or sometimes even greater devaluations were made, and the effect was lost.

Fixed Par Values

After the outcome of World War II became relatively certain, representatives of the new United Nations Organization met in 1944 at Bretton Woods,

New Hampshire, to make plans for a postwar monetary system. Experience with the old gold standard and fluctuating rates was unsatisfactory to most of the delegates, and they made a new approach to the problems of international exchange. They established the International Monetary Fund (IMF) and developed a table of exchange rates (fixed par values). These form the basis of today's international financial system.

Members of the IMF each contribute gold and a given amount of their own currencies to a central fund. The amount a nation contributes is proportional to the size of its GNP and the volume of international trade in which it engages. From this fund, a member nation may borrow either gold or the kinds of foreign exchange it needs whenever it has a balance of payments deficit. The nation pays back the loan when it has an equilibrium or a surplus in its balance of payments.

The values of all members' currencies are defined in terms of United States dollars and gold, with the official price of gold being set at $35 per ounce. Under the system of fixed par values, it is the responsibility of members to keep their currencies within 1 percent above or below the official exchange rate on the international money markets. They must do this through exchange stabilization operations if necessary. A member country can devalue or evalue its currency only after it consults with the IMF and its members.

Foreign money is exchanged for United States dollars in Minneapolis, Minnesota. Members of the International Monetary Fund must keep the value of their currencies at an official exchange rate.

The fund has prevented a return of the confused conditions of the prewar era. It has allowed nations to make up for disequilibrium in their balance of payments without causing domestic recession or a round of competitive currency devaluation. Changes in exchange rates have been orderly; they have occurred with the consultation and cooperation of major trading partners, and they have been relatively rare. The

John Maynard Keynes. He was the first economist to propose the creation of Supplementary Drawing Rights.

IMF has had two other important functions: it has provided a permanent place where nations can discuss their monetary problems, and it has supplied expert technical assistance. The IMF also has proved that it is able to adjust to new monetary developments.

The amount of world commerce has tripled since 1945. This has required larger contributions of gold and national currencies to the IMF to finance occasional imbalances and currency crises. Members have recently increased their contributions to the fund, and they have also agreed to a new kind of international liquidity, the SDRs. These initials stand for *Supplementary Drawing Rights*. The agreement allows the IMF to issue, for time to time, SDR certificates. These will be acceptable among members for payment of debts which come from balance of payments deficits or from international loans. SDRs have also been called "paper gold," because they replace real gold in international transactions. After a century, the international monetary system has developed a way of increasing money reserves without relying on the relatively small amount of existing gold ore.

This is particularly significant because the volume of trade has increased far more rapidly than the output of gold. In recent years there has been a tremendous increase in industrial demand for the yellow metal. The competition between monetary and manufacturing uses has made it difficult to maintain the low official price of $35 per ounce. In order to keep the fixed rate of exchange system, two markets for gold have been set up. One of these, the official monetary market, maintains the $35 price and includes only central banks. The other is a free gold market, in which the price fluctuates in response to the forces of supply and demand.

5

Toward Freer Trade

Many nations of the world have formulated trade policies which promote the growth of specialization and free trade. Especially encouraging are foreign aid to developing nations, reduction of tariffs and other trade restrictions, and establishment of trade or customs unions.

Foreign Aid

In the movement toward freer trade, some nations are likely to gain more of the increased world output than others. This is because the more a nation produces, the more it will have to trade for what it needs; the greater efficiency it has, the greater will be its gains from trade. The size and the resources of a country are largely the result of political and historical circumstances, and the efficient use of those resources is in large part due to the skills and attitudes of the nation. In many nations these factors have combined to produce substantial economic development. Switzerland, Belgium, and Denmark, for example, have developed their location and resources more than Tibet, Portugal, or Peru. Even though the gain from free trade does tend to favor the more efficient economies, their surpluses of capital and technology, in turn, seek out new opportunities in less developed, lower cost regions of the globe.

The economic progress of underdeveloped regions has, in fact, been a major concern to the more efficient economies since the end of World War II. The Bretton Woods Conference in 1944 created another organization, the International Bank for Reconstruction and Development (IBRD). Its purpose was to provide long term, low interest loans to countries in order to rebuild after the war, and later on, to provide credit for economic development. Since that time, other national and international agencies have also been created to help underdeveloped nations make economic growth.

The main contributor to this international effort has been the United States, which has granted and lent more than $110 billion since 1946. The spending of tax dollars for foreign aid has often been criticized. Much of the money has been spent carelessly and without attention to whether the dollars would yield real increases of output or higher living standards.

Building the Kainji Dam in northern Nigeria. Much of the dam was financed by a loan from the International Bank for Reconstruction and Development.

Nevertheless, the principle of aid to developing nations has three strong economic reasons behind it.

Statistics indicate that richer nations are better customers internationally; they buy more, and they contribute more to world output. The greater the growth rate developing nations can manage, the sooner they will be able to participate more importantly in world trade.

Secondly, the underdeveloped world is a source of many raw materials needed by industrial nations. Foreign aid dollars will increase the efficiency of mining or producing these raw materials, and thereby lower their price in the world market. This will result in a lower price for the manufactured goods of which the raw materials are a part.

Finally, foreign aid and technical assistance bring people together. Common interests lead to a sharing of ideas and cultures. The developing countries can learn much from the developed in matters of production, management, and modern methods; the developed countries can benefit from an exposure to the ideas and traditions of the less mechanized, less automated societies. With the Western knowledge of economic efficiency may also go the concepts of individual freedom and democratic institutions. Doubtless, a world sharing these common ideals would be more peaceful and more compatible with our own national goals.

Tariffs

The United States has been the leader in a second important trade policy, the reduction of tariffs. The reduction began with the Reciprocal Trade Agreements Act of 1934. This law reversed the high tariff trend that had been building since 1920 and had reached its peak with the Hawley-Smoot Act of 1930. The Hawley-Smoot Act had raised average duties collected on imports to 52.8 percent of their value. Working bilaterally (making agreements with one nation at a time), the United States reduced average duties to 37.3 percent between 1934 and 1939.

Two central concepts of the Reciprocal Trade Act of 1934 have proven especially valuable, not only in negotiations reshaping the tariff structure of the United States, but also in international tariff bargaining. The first of these is the idea of *reciprocity* — two nations agree to lower tariffs on each other's products. That is, if one party is willing to reduce duties by 10 percent on a given kind of imports, the other country will reciprocate; it will match the 10 percent tariff cut on its imports from the first party. The other concept is that of the *most-favored nation.* If two nations agree to reciprocal tariff reductions of 5 percent and either party thereafter agrees to a greater reduction, say 8 percent, with a third nation, then the first contracting nation also gets an 8 percent reduction. The countries which sign a treaty are entitled to get the same tariff rates, on any given product, as the most-favored nation.

These principles were included as an essential feature of the General Agreement on Tariffs and Trade (GATT) ratified by 23 nations in 1947. The GATT has a present membership of over 60 nations, who meet every two years to bargain down trade barriers. Tariffs, quotas, discriminatory trade practices, and pricing agreements are all given close examination,

One of the first meetings of the members of the General Agreement on Tariffs and Trade, August 17, 1948. Over 60 nations now belong to the GATT.

and most of them have been greatly reduced since 1947. Table Three indicates the impact of the GATT on United States average duty rates.

Table Three

Year	Tariff Law	Duties Collected, percent of import value
1947	GATT	15.3
1963	GATT Trade Expansion Act of 1962	11.9

When foreign competition becomes keen, there is always a renewal of a desire for protective trade barriers, and political pressure is brought to bear on foreign economic policy. With the recovery of Western Europe in the years after 1953, many United States products were no longer competitively priced on the world market. Consequently, a number of escape clauses were added to the Trade Agreements Act of 1934. These allow tariff reductions to be suspended if a domestic industry is suffering from foreign competition, and remove certain products from tariff negotiations altogether if they are considered essential to national defense. These protectionist measures have only rarely been used, but the greater the foreign competition, the louder will be the cry for their use.

Two factors have contributed to an increase of imports into the United States. First, the high level of productive efficiency of industry in Japan and West

Germany has given these nations low cost comparative advantage in many manufactured goods. Second, many countries in the world have improved their trade positions by joining together in customs unions and free trade areas.

Customs Unions

The most successful customs union is the European Economic Community (EEC), better known as the Common Market. Six nations of Western Europe — France, Italy, Belgium, The Netherlands, Luxembourg, and West Germany — signed the Treaty of Rome in 1958. They set out on a program to do away with all tariff barriers among themselves, to erect a common tariff wall to outsiders, and to work toward complete economic union. This amounted to an agreement to create a free trade area among the member nations. The growth rate and volume of trade among the six has set the pace for the rest of the world. It has given further proof that specialization and free trade result in greater output and efficiency.

The experience of the EEC also shows that larger markets lead to economies of scale; countries produce more goods because they can sell more, and increased production leads to greater efficiency and lower prices. Their united position also gives them greater competitive power and a stronger bargaining position in international conferences. The Common Market has moved to coordinate its agricultural policy and its monetary, fiscal, tax, and antitrust policies. It even

NETHERLANDS

BELGIUM

GREAT
BRITAIN

N

LUXEMBOURG

W. GERMANY

FRANCE

SWITZ.

AUS.

PORTUGAL

SPAIN

ITALY

■ COMMON MARKET COUNTRIES

plans to have a common currency in the future.

Other customs unions — the European Free Trade Association, the Latin American Common Market, and the Central American Free Trade Association — have less ambitious goals, yet their limited cooperation in tariff reduction has yielded greater gains in trade for their members.

As a rule, the fewer barriers among trading partners, the greater will be the gains from trade. This has been true historically in every application of the principles of free trade and specialization. The best example is the United States. After the Revolutionary War each of the 13 original states had its own tariffs; in addition, some still used different currencies. This is very much like the conditions of international trade today. Prosperity for the states was uneven, and growth was slower than in most of the colonial period. After the ratification of the Constitution, which removed all state trade barriers, there was a surge of interstate commerce. The easy flow of goods and services allowed a higher degree of specialization than before, and it began a period of growth that has moved the country forward for nearly 200 years.

6

The Future of
International Trade

International cooperation in financial matters and
in tariff reduction has taken giant strides since the
end of World War II. The formation of customs unions and common markets, which create large areas of
free trade, is very encouraging. Even so, there are a
number of issues that threaten past progress in this
area, and represent difficult obstacles to be overcome
before freer trade and a sound international monetary
system are realities.

Increased foreign competition is likely to bring back requests for more protection, in the form of higher tariffs, quotas, and restrictive barriers. If the benefits of trade are to be gained these requests must be ignored. Each country must give assistance to its industries being hurt by foreign competition, so that they can become more efficient and able to compete in the world markets. If this is not possible, aid must be given to encourage the transfer of the resources involved to areas of production in which there will be genuine comparative advantage.

Bargaining down tariffs has become more and more difficult as the least contested duties have been removed. Now only the most sensitive ones remain, and with them the host of non-tariff barriers, some of which are difficult to detect. What this means is that further reduction of trade barriers is likely to be progressively harder to achieve.

The international monetary system has survived half a dozen crises since the organization of the IMF, but it is by no means completely secure. Lack of cooperation among major trading nations, attempts to avoid the rules that govern the system, and widespread use of foreign exchange controls to correct internal economic problems are all threats to the continued functioning of present international monetary arrangements. The strongest reasons for optimism in this area are the creation of paper gold to relieve the shortage of liquidity and reserves, and the great ease with which present financial institutions have met new conditions as they arise.

Economists have been very much encouraged by the increase in free trade due to the establishment of the Common Market and other regional groupings. Their great efficiency and prosperity will benefit all trading nations, unless each trade organization uses its new bargaining power and economic strength to isolate itself behind its own protective barriers. The principles of competition and free markets, which have been for so long the standard of efficiency and progress within the economy of the United States, will give all nations the greatest benefits from international trade.

Glossary

artificial barriers — Restrictions set up by individual countries which interfere with a free exchange of goods and services between nations.

capital account — The section of the balance of payments statement which records capital that has entered or left the country.

currency — A medium of exchange; money in actual use, generally referring to paper money.

current account — The section of the balance of payments statement which records income and expenditures on exports and imports.

cyclical disequilibrium — A deficit or surplus in a nation's balance of payments which requires monetary or fiscal adjustment because it results from internal, or business cycle conditions.

devaluation — A reduction of the value of one country's currency in terms of other currencies. A nation devalues its currency to reduce a balance of payments deficit, because devaluation tends to lower the cost of its exports and raise the cost of foreign imports.

errors and omissions — The section of the balance of payments statement which estimates unrecorded exchanges of goods and capital.

equilibrium — A condition of balance in a nation's international trade. Money spent on foreign products and in foreign countries equals money received from foreign countries and foreign tourists.

evaluation — Raising the value of a nation's currency in terms of other currencies. Evaluation tends to reduce an export balance of trade because it makes a nation's exports more expensive and foreign imports less expensive.

exchange rate — The relative value of one currency in terms of another.

factoral immobility — The inability of the factors of production — land, labor, capital, technology, and entrepreneurship — to move from one country to another.

favorable balance of trade — A condition of having more exports than imports. This actually may not benefit a country in the long run because it raises the amount of money within an economy, which may in turn cause inflation.

foreign exchange — Currency of different nations used in international trade.

interdependency — A basic cause of trade between nations. Every nation depends, to some extent, on foreign imports to provide goods not otherwise available. And every nation thus also depends on income from its exports.

international liquidity — Anything which acts as a medium of exchange between nations. Gold, stable currencies, promises to pay, and SDRs serve as international liquidity.

mercantilism — An economic policy which attempts to create an export balance of trade in order to build up a nation's wealth.

most-favored nation — A concept in international tariff agreements. A country gives to all nations the terms it has given to the most-favored nation; that is, the one which has received the best terms.

price-specie-flow mechanism — A method of adjusting balance of payments disequilibria, in use before World War I. A disequilibrium caused gold to flow in or out of a country, which tended to bring prices to the level of prices in other countries. This automatically corrected the disequilibrium.

quota — A limit placed on the quantity in which a specific product may be imported or exported.

reciprocity — A concept in international tariff agreements. Two countries agree to similar tariff policy on certain of each other's products.

socio-cultural differences — Restrictions on international trade caused by differences in language and customs.

structural disequilibrium — A basic weakness in a nation's economy which results in a long term balance of payments deficit or surplus.

Supplementary Drawing Rights — A special currency created by the International Monetary Fund. Members of the fund may use SDRs instead of gold to finance balance of payments deficits.

tariffs — Taxes levied on goods imported from other countries.

temporary disequilibrium — A balance of payments surplus or deficit of short duration caused by circumstances not likely to be repeated.

unfavorable balance of trade — A condition of having more imports than exports. This may result in a deficit in a nation's balance of payments.

Index

the author . . .

Kenneth H. Smith is an associate professor of economics at Hunter College, City University of New York. He has been an economic consultant to private firms and also several United Nations agencies. Professor Smith received both his bachelor's and his master's degrees from Southern Methodist University and his Ph.D. from the University of Oklahoma. Dr. Smith is coauthor of *Economics,* an economics text for college students.

The Real World Books

*We specialize in producing quality books for
young people. For a complete list please write*

LERNER PUBLICATIONS COMPANY
241 First Avenue North, Minneapolis, Minnesota 55401